SHOTOKAN K

Patrick Stephens Limited, part of Thorsons, a division of the Collins Publishing
Group, has published authoritative, quality books for enthusiasts for more than
twenty years. During that time the company has established a reputation as
one of the world's leading publishers of books on aviation, maritime, military,
model-making, motor cycling, motoring, motor racing, railway and railway
modelling, and sports and pastimes subjects. Readers or authors with
suggestions for books they would like to see published are invited to write to:
The Editorial Director, Patrick Stephens Limited, Thorsons Publishing Group,
Wellingborough, Northants, NN8 2RQ.

SHOTOKAN KARATE

David Mitchell

Patrick Stephens Limited

First published in 1990

British Library Cataloguing in Publication Data
Mitchell, David, *1944-*
Shotokan Karate.
1. Karate
I. Title
796.8'153

ISBN 1-85260-279-1

Patrick Stephens Limited is part of the
Thorsons Publishing Group, Wellingborough,
Northamptonshire NN8 2RQ, England.

Printed by Bath Press, Bath, Avon
Typesetting by MJL Limited, Hitchin, Hertfordshire.

1   3   5   7   9   10   8   6   4   2

Contents

Dedication   7
Acknowledgements   9
Shotokan Karate   11
The Shotokan Club   15
The White Belt Syllabus   19
The Second White Belt Syllabus   47
The Yellow Belt Syllabus   53
The Orange Belt Syllabus   67
The Green Belt Syllabus   81
The Purple Belt Syllabus   93
The First Brown Belt Syllabus   99
The Second and First Brown Belt Syllabus   107
Glossary   111

Dedication

I dedicate this book to Bernard Whelan who, in my opinion, has done more to further the development of martial arts in general, and karate in particular, than anyone else in Britain. Barney, as he is known, is the Chairman of the Martial Arts Commission, of the British Karate Federation and of the Scottish Karate Board of Control.

When someone asks me to define a martial artist, I never think in terms of power or skill but only of those core characteristics which are developed by the true martial artist — wisdom, patience, humility, kindness and loyalty. Measured on that rather exacting scale, Bernard Whelan emerges as one of the finest martial artists I have ever known.

Acknowledgements

It is a great pleasure for me to acknowledge the assistance provided by Paul Perry 5th Dan, Michael Gorman 4th Dan and Barry Shearer 4th Dan of the Jin Sei Kai in the production of this book. Paul is one of the few senior British Shotokan black belts to analyse and lucidly interpret the techniques of his school. He was therefore the ideal person to advise the author on the finer points of technique.

Shotokan Karate

The meaning of Shotokan Karate

Shoto is the nickname of the late Gichin Funakoshi — 'The Father of Japanese Karate'. More will be said of him later in this chapter, but for now just note that Funakoshi considered himself a poet and took the pen-name **Shoto**, meaning 'Waving Pines'. **Kan** is a commonly used word in Japanese martial art practice meaning 'club'. **Shotokan** therefore means 'Shoto's Club'.

Do not confuse Shotokan with **Shotokai**, because the two are quite different. Shotokai is a branch school of Shotokan founded by one of Funakoshi's senior students, Shigeru Egami. This is very like the original version of Shotokan as taught by Funakoshi.

This gradual changing of the way in which a style is practised is quite natural because it recognizes the contributions made by those who follow in the founder's footsteps. New masters bring their own personal interpretations to enrich the original inspiration, so, as time passes, the tradition grows in knowledge.

Kara is a Japanese word used to describe the China of the Tang dynasty (CE 618-907). However, a desire to promote karate as wholly Japanese led to the adoption of a different kanji character. Although still pronounced 'kara', it now means 'empty'. **Te** simply means 'hand', so 'empty hand' can be taken to mean that karate uses no weapons. Yet we know that this is not strictly the case, for although no weapons are taught in the Shotokan syllabus, earlier schools of karate did use them. In fact, the unarmed portion of karate was originally the less important part of training.

Karate's name change was made by Funakoshi, and such was his great prestige that other teachers followed suit. Funakoshi was much impressed with the **Kodokan judo** developed from **Jiu jitsu** by Jigoro Kano. This new development shifted the object of practice from being able to defeat adversaries to being able to defeat one's own ego. Seen from this perspective, **kara** as 'empty' suggests an absence of preconception or influence — a way of acting without malice or hysteria.

The founding of Shotokan karate

Gichin Funakoshi is credited not only with introducing Shotokan to the Japanese mainland but also with introducing and sponsoring karate itself! Okinawa was regarded by mainland Japanese as a rural backwater, so the fighting art it evolved was somewhat tainted by the contempt in which Japanese held the Okinawans. Nevertheless, Funakoshi succeeded in promoting karate and it is largely through his efforts alone that the first Japanese governing body of karate was set up.

Funakoshi was born in Shuri, the capital of Okinawa, in 1868. He was a weak child so his family sent him to learn **Okinawan kempo** ('Okinawan boxing') under Masters Azato and Itosu. He studied assiduously and became known as a competent practitioner.

In 1902 he gave a demonstration of Okinawan kempo to Shintaro Ozawa, the Commissioner of Okinawan Schools. This led ultimately to the incorporation of karate into the national school curriculum in 1903. In 1906 Funakoshi gave the first public demonstration of karate.

In 1912, Funakoshi was selected by a meeting of Okinawan karate masters to give a demonstration before the Admiral of the Japanese Imperial Fleet. This stimulated interest on the mainland, so in 1917 he visited Japan and gave a demonstration at the **Butokuden** ('Hall of Ancient Martial Virtue'). Afterwards he returned to Okinawa and began full-time promotion of Okinawan kempo.

He persuaded the Okinawan masters to set up a liaison body named **Okinawan Shobukai**. This body subsequently chose Funakoshi to demonstrate karate to the Japanese Crown Prince during his visit to Shuri Castle. Afterwards Funakoshi left Okinawa for the Japanese mainland and gave a demonstration for Jigoro Kano. Kano was so impressed that he asked Funakoshi to teach him some basic karate techniques.

In 1922 Funakoshi opened the Meisei Juku dojo in Suidobata, Tokyo. Two years later he opened a karate club at Keio University. The Tokyo University Karate Club followed in 1926, after which came clubs in the universities of Chuo, Takushoku, Nihon, Meiji and Waseda. Today there are more than 200 collegiate karate clubs registered with the Japan Student Karate Federation.

In 1928 Funakoshi gave a demonstration for the Royal Family in the Dainei-sen Hall in the Palace Grounds. In 1936 his students raised sufficient funds to build the first karate dojo. This was named the **Shotokan**, but it was destroyed in 1945 during an air-raid.

Funakoshi was appointed Chief Instructor to the **Nippon Karatedo Renmei** ('Japan Karate Association') in 1949.

Funakoshi died at the age of 89 on 25 April 1957, leaving behind a monument to his endeavours — the largest school of karate in the world, and one of the four major schools of Japanese karate.

Shotokan karate in Britain

Shotokan karate was introduced to Britain during 1965. The first senior high grade to begin teaching here was Hirokazu Kanazawa, then a 6th dan black belt, and he was followed by Keinosuke Enoeda, also of the same grade. Kanazawa subsequently left Britain for the continent, though he still returns periodically. The first Shotokan-practising association was The Karate Union of Great Britain and that body still exists today, though now there are more than 70 other associations which practise Shotokan.

Interestingly, Shotokai was the very first genuine karate organization to be set up in Britain and the Chief Instructor then, as now, is Mitsusuke Harada.

Characteristics of Shotokan karate

Shotokan karate is based upon the Okinawan **Shorin ryu** schools, and uses long, deep stances and powerful thrusting movements. A great deal of emphasis is placed upon the withdrawing of the non-active limb since this produces a powerful 'pulley effect', which we will discuss later.

Shotokan is a forceful style and this is echoed in its strong advances and unremitting attacks. Much attention is paid to the notion of 'focusing' the power of a technique so that it literally explodes on the target. The techniques themselves tend to involve long movements. A punch, for example, starts from a cocked position on the hip and concludes with the arm fully outstretched. Blocks also use generous movements to sweep a wide area free of incoming attack.

Shotokan is most noted for its large syllabus of **kata**. These are training forms of often great complexity. More will be said about them later. Shotokan has taken kata from many different early styles and incorporated them into its syllabus, changing each one to the characteristic Shotokan format in the process.

The Shotokan Club

If you have not yet begun training, the first thing to do is to join a good club. The address of your nearest club can be obtained from the Martial Arts Commission, 1st Floor Broadway House, 15-16 Deptford Broadway, London SE8 4PE (enclose a stamped addressed envelope if you want a prompt reply). The telephone number is 081-691 3433. The Commission has a current register of all the authentic clubs in Britain and will be able to help you.

Not all karate clubs are staffed by competent coaches. In fact, anyone can buy a black belt and set up as a coach. Some clubs are run by students who dropped out of training at an early stage; they may have learned a little but will not be qualified to teach. Unfortunately such people will have no problem in joining an unscrupulous karate association which is not affiliated to the governing body. Associations which are registered with the Commission do produce skilled **karateka** (people who practise karate) and those students who become interested in teaching can take a coaching examination. This ensures that they can pass on their knowledge both efficiently and safely.

Karate is not one of the most expensive activities to take up. There is an initial joining fee when you become a member of the club and thereafter a nightly mat fee. You must also register annually through the club with the club's parent association. This includes the cost of a Martial Arts Commission licence, which incorporates a valuable personal accident/third party insurance policy.

You will need a karate suit (**karategi**), but don't buy one before joining a club, as many club coaches can supply a good one more cheaply than one bought from a sports shop. Buy a size too large because karategis continue to shrink when washed. Each comes with a white belt and this will be suitable as a starting colour for most clubs. However, some may require you to start with a red belt — but keep the white belt anyway, because you will need it after your first grading.

At some stage you will need to buy a set of fist protectors, known colloquially as 'mitts'. In all probability, these will also be available through your club. Choose a pair which leaves the thumbs free and which has no more than 1cm of padding over the knuckles. Shin pads are also useful, but make sure they fit comfortably and securely around your calves. 'Flip-flop' sandals are worth buying, especially if you must walk a distance between the changing room and the training area, and a tracksuit will keep you warm during lulls in training.

Shotokan karate training is broken down into nine units known as **kyu** grades. Each unit contains a cross-section of practice, requiring more and more skill as you approach black belt. Each kyu grade is identified by a coloured belt, and the following sequence is typical:

Novice grade	3 months	Red belt
9th kyu	3 months	White belt
8th kyu	3 months	White belt/ black tab
7th kyu	3 months	Yellow belt
6th kyu	3 months	Orange belt
5th kyu	3 months	Green belt
4th kyu	3 months	Purple belt
3rd kyu	3 months	Brown belt/ white line
2nd kyu	6 months	Brown belt
1st kyu	6 months	Brown belt/ black line

It therefore takes approximately 36 months to progress through the grades to black belt, this figure being based upon twice-weekly training, with each session lasting a minimum of 90 minutes. Additionally you should attend weekend courses which cover specialized subjects in greater detail. Winter and summer residential courses are excellent because they increase your circle of friends and provide intensive training.

Do not train only during lessons. Train at home and your technique will improve more rapidly. Remember — successful karate training is based upon endless repe-tition, so the more you practise the better you will become.

The coach monitors your training and corrects mistakes by repositioning your arms and legs. Try to *feel* the corrected position, so you develop an awareness of what you are doing. This reduces the need for external correction and means that you will do better at grading examinations.

Provided you miss few or no lessons, you will learn all the required techniques well inside the grading period. Your coach will advise you when to take the grading and this generally means that despite any feelings of unpreparedness you may have, your techniques are up to scratch. It only remains for you to go out on the practice area and do your best. Few sensible coaches fail students!

A typical night's training in Shotokan karate

Get changed from your working clothes into your karategi and track suit, then go to the door of the training hall (**dojo**). Pause there and turn towards the senior grade. If no senior grade is present, face the centre of the room and perform a standing bow. Bring your heels together, place the flats of your hands against the front of your thighs, then incline your head and upper body forward in a smooth action. Pause at the lowest point, then return once more to an upright position. Kick your flip-flops off and go on to the training floor.

Warm up by running on the spot, or by gently performing karate techniques, but don't undertake any strenuous or explosive action at this time. Your body will take a short time to prepare for training and it is best to warm up gradually. Slip off your track suit when you feel warm.

When all the students have arrived, the class senior will call them to order. Everyone stands in lines according to their grade, so check to see which line is yours and join it midway along its length. This will allow you to compare what you are doing with your more experienced neighbours. The senior grade then takes the class through a programme of exercises designed to loosen up every joint in the body, and to narrow your attention down to the evening's training. An effective training session consists of three exercise periods which are:

- The warm-up, to prepare you for training;

- Body preparation, to improve your fitness;

- The cool-down, to return you to normal levels of activity.

When the class is thoroughly prepared, the senior student joins the lines and the coach takes his position at the head. Use this time to adjust your karategi. The senior student calls out a series of commands. These are:

- **Seiza!** Drop down on to your right knee, bring your left knee in and kneel down with back straight and ankles fully extended. Place the palms of your hands on the top of your thighs;

- **Sensei-ni-rei!** Slide your hands forward and off the front of your knees. Incline you upper body but keep looking forward. Pause at the lowest point, then return to an upright position;

- **Kiritsu!** Lift your left knee, then the

right, resuming a standing position with heels together and feet splayed, palms flat on the front of your thighs;

- **Rei!** Perform a standing bow, and you are now ready to begin training.

The above sequence of commands is also repeated at the end of the training session.

Different schools sometimes introduce an additional kneeling bow, either towards a portrait or saying of the school's founder, or between the members of the class.

If you arrive late and the lesson has already begun, warm up unobtrusively and then perform the kneeling bow. Remain in the kneeling position and wait to be summoned on to the mat.

If all this seems rather strange, remember that karate is not merely a leisure or sporting activity. Its roots go a long way back into Japanese culture, and these rituals illustrate and underline the courtesy and respect which are integral to good karate practice.

Training in Shotokan karate falls into the following categories:

- Basic techniques (**kihon**): these are the individual punches (**zuki**), kicks (**keri**) and strikes (**ate**);

- Blocks (**uke**): blocking techniques to prevent an attack from reaching its target;

- Combination techniques (**renraku waza**): these are a series of basic techniques, kicks and blocks performed without breaks in between;

- **Kata**: there is no commonly used English equivalent for this. Katas are whole series of combination techniques performed at different speeds and in different directions;

- Prearranged sparring (**gohon/sanbon/ippon kumite**): this is work with a partner — he performs set attacks and you respond to them in a prearranged manner;

- Semi-free sparring (**jiu ippon kumite**): this is advanced partner work in which the attack is delivered in a more realistic way and greater latitude is allowed in responding to it;

- Basic sparring (**kihon kumite**): despite the title, this type of sparring requires a much higher standard of practice;

- Free sparring (**jiu kumite**): this allows the free use of non-prohibited techniques in a realistic way.

Each lesson aims to cover as many topics as possible, though additional classes are given to kata because it takes a lot of time.

The following rules apply in any karate training hall:

- Do not smoke or eat in the training hall;

- Do not chew gum;

- Do not lark about;

- Do not talk loudly, or behave in an unseemly manner;

- Keep your karategi clean and in good repair;

- Do not sprawl over the floor during breaks. Sit with legs crossed, or in a kneeling position;

- Do not lean against walls or pillars, but stand straight with your arms to your sides;

- Stop what you are doing when the coach calls for attention;

- Talk only when it is necessary to exchange relevant training information;

- Treat your training partner with respect and consideration at all times.

Do not use karate skills in the street. In the hands of an expert, karate can be very dangerous, and even a small miscalculation — such as may happen in the heat of a fight — can lead to tragedy. The true karateka avoids this by walking away from trouble.

Remember the old maxim: **Karate-ni sentenashi** — 'In karate, one *never* strikes first.'

The White Belt Syllabus

Introduction

The white belt, or 9th kyu syllabus, is the first step on the path leading to black belt, and is perhaps the most challenging grade since everything is new. The relentless repetition of basic technique is enough to drive away all but the keenest students. Maybe this is not altogether a bad thing since it gets rid of unsuitable persons before they can learn the more practical techniques of karate.

Repetition is the *only* way to develop skill, and the harder you work at this grade, the easier the next becomes.

Preliminary training

Before entering into the syllabus proper, you must learn how to make a fist and how to punch effectively. Open your hand out fully and then fold down the fingers until they touch the bar of flesh running along the top of the palm. Close the fist, locking the index and middle fingers by folding the thumb across. Look at the top of your fist

and you will see that it is uneven — the knuckles do not lie all in one line. In recognition of this, Shotokan karate uses only the knuckles of the index and middle fingers. This has the additional benefit of concentrating impact force through a small area, so punches become more powerful.

Use a light punching bag to check that you are striking with the correct part of the knuckles — punch gently at first! You may find that you cannot fold your fingers in tight enough, so the fist strikes the bag with the middle knuckles. This is a common fault and must be corrected by repeated bag work, or by press-ups on closed fists (but avoid damaging your knuckle joints by doing the press-ups from a slightly padded surface).

Bag work will also show how to position your wrist joint, so impact does not cause it to flex or twist. You will discover that the best impacts are made when the supporting bones of the two leading knuckles are in a straight line, through the wrist, with the two bones in the forearm — any deviation from this straight line will cause the wrist to bend. Most karate punches use a turning action of the forearm, so the fist twists palm-downwards as contact is made. It is

Figure 1 *The stance known as* **fudodachi** *places the feet a shoulder-width apart. The fists are carried in front of the thighs.*

Figure 2 *Open your left hand and fold it across your chest, beneath the extended right arm.*

not necessary to use this action when punching the bag.

Basic techniques

Basic punch

The basic punching action is practised from a feet-apart stance known as **fudo-dachi**. Step to the side with the left foot, then with the right, until both are approximately a shoulder-width apart. The feet are turned slightly outwards and the closed fists are carried in front of the thighs (**1**).

Extend your right arm and twist the fist so that the palm turns downwards. Do not let your shoulder lift or move forward behind the action. The extended fist should be in the mid-line of the body. Open your left hand and bring your forearm across your chest, just below the extended arm (**2**). Draw back your right fist to the hip, rotating it palm-upwards as it comes to rest. Move at exactly the same speed with your left hand, extending it out and turning the palm forward (**3**).

On the command, withdraw your left hand and close it into a fist. Simultaneously thrust out the right, so they pass each other at the midway point (**4**). As the right elbow extends, the left flexes, then, in the last few instants, both fists suddenly rotate so the right fist turns palm-downwards and the left palm-upwards (**5**) — this action *must* be simultaneous. Keep both fists relaxed until this moment, then clench them tightly as imaginary impact occurs.

Relax your shoulders and draw back your right fist whilst extending your open left hand once more. Be prepared to repeat the punch up to ten times on one side, then change your arms over and practise punch-

Figure 3 *Extend your left arm and turn the palm forward.*

Figure 4 *Your fists pass each other at the midway point of the punch.*

Figure 5 *Both fists rotate as the punch comes to a stop.*

ing with your left fist. This part of the syllabus is known as **kara zuki**.

All the punches which you will subsequently learn are based upon this combination of pull-back with punching action. Unfortunately most beginners concentrate only on the punch and ignore the pull-back. This produces incorrect technique which, if it is not put right at an early stage, is more difficult to eradicate later. I therefore recommend that you practise this action using your karate belt.

Take up your stance facing a firmly anchored pole. Pass your belt around it and grasp an end in each hand. Adjust the free length of belt held so when one fist is extended, you have enough belt to pull the other end back to your hip. Begin slowly by putting all of your energy into pulling back the withdrawing fist. Speed up the action as you become used to it and this will soon generate the right feel.

Examine the way you are punching and see if there is any way to make the punch stronger without leaning your shoulders into the action. Take your hip back slightly as you withdraw a fist and then twist it forward a few degrees as that same fist extends, but do not exaggerate this movement. Then do the same with your shoulders, but again, do not move more than a couple of degrees or so. Allow the shoulders to drop slightly as the punching arm reaches full extension — this locks the arm and gives it extra rigidity.

Reverse punch

This is the second technique in the syllabus. Step a full pace forward with your left leg, or a full pace back with your right. I shall have more to say about the stance used a little further on. Extend your left hand as before, drawing the right back to

Figures 6 and 7 *Step forward and extend your left hand. The right hip is withdrawn.*

8

your hip (**6** and **7**). On the command, draw back your left hand as you thrust forward the right fist (**8** and **9**). Notice how the right hip moves forward to help power the action.

The left hand closes into a fist and both rotate, so the right turns palm-downwards and the left palm-upwards (**10** and **11**). Then extend and open your left hand once more and make ready to repeat the sequence. This is known as **gyaku zuki**, or 'reverse punch', so named because the leading foot of the stance and the extended fist are always opposite. If the left foot

Figures 8 and 9 *Twist your punching hip forward as you withdraw your left hand.*

9

Figures 10 and 11 *Rotate your fists as the punch comes to a stop. Note the involvement of the right hip in the overall action.*

leads, then the right fist will be used for the punch. Perform reverse punch five times on each arm.

Lunge punch

Stand with your feet a shoulder-width apart and your hands closed into fists. On the command, follow this sequence:

- Bend your knees, fully extend your right fist and fold the left arm so the fist rests lightly on the top of your right shoulder (**12** and **13**);

- Step forward a pace and a half with your left leg. Fully straighten your right leg, using this action to thrust the left

foot forward. Use the pulley principle described above to pull back your right hand to the hip while straightening the left arm (**14** and **15**). The left arm

Figures 12 and 13 *Fold the left arm so that the fist rests on the top of your right shoulder.*

sweeps diagonally forward and down in the action known as 'lower parry' (**gedan barai**). This action will be described in greater detail a little further on.

The stance you have just taken up is known as left 'forward stance', or **zenkutsudachi**.

It has the following characteristics:

● The right knee is fully straightened;

Figures 14 and 15 *Bring your left arm down and across your body in the action known as 'lower parry'. This is the starting point for most basic techniques.*

Figures 16 and 17 *Keep the extended arm perfectly still and ensure that you do not straighten your knees as you step.*

- The left knee is bent so that it overlies the toes;

- The right foot is twisted to face forwards as far as is comfortable;

- The left foot points directly forwards;

- The left foot not only lies in front of the right, but it also lies to the left side, so the stance has an element of sidestep necessary to give stability;

- The right hip is drawn back slightly, in which position it is said to be 'cocked';
- The shoulders are relaxed and the head is held high;
- The right fist is palm-upwards facing on the right hip. The left fist is turned palm-downwards;
- The left fist lies above the left knee.

Use a mirror to check all these points if you are training at home. Take special note of the side-step, which should not be so narrow as to make the stance unstable, nor should it be so wide as to open your groin to the opponent's attack.

Step forward with the right foot, so that:

- The right foot advances a pace and a half, accelerating all the way;
- The left leg remains bent as you step (**16** and **17**), to prevent you from giving the appearance of bobbing up and down;
- Your shoulders remain relaxed and do not hunch;
- Your left arm remains extended and does not waggle around (**18**);
- The left arm is pulled back **only** when weight descends on the right foot — neither before nor after. Use the pull-back of the left arm to power a punch with the right fist;
- At the conclusion of the step forward, the right arm is fully extended and the left lies on the hip (**19** and **20**).

The two hardest things are keeping a degree of side-step in the stance and

Figure 18 *Continue the step forward.*

punching at the right time to make use of the energy generated by your advancing body. Typically, novices punch too early and throw themselves off balance, or they wait too long and punch once they have stopped moving, so momentum is lost.

Rising block

Repeat the lunge punch (**oi zuki**) until you run out of space, then step back and perform a series of retreating rising blocks,

using the forearm (**age uke**). Follow this sequence from left lunge punch:

● Draw back your left foot and extend your left arm above and in front of your head. Open your hand and turn it so the palm faces forwards (**21** and **22**). This is to set up the pulley action that will power the block proper;

● Continue to step back with your left foot and pull your left arm diagonally down across the front of your chest. Use this to power the action of the right arm as the latter thrusts diagonally upwards. The two arms pass each other at the midway point, creating a

Figures 19 and 20 *Complete the step forward and punch. Time the punch so impact occurs even as the step forward completes.*

Figures 21 and 22 *Keep your knees bent to avoid bobbing up and down as you step back. Extend your left arm and open the fingers.*

Figures 23 and 24 *Because your arms are moving at exactly the same speed, the forearms cross each other at the midway point in a characteristic 'x-block' configuration.*

characteristic 'x' with the forearms (**23** and **24**);

● Continue stepping back with the left foot until it takes up its final position. At the same time, complete the pulley action, drawing your left arm to your hip and thrusting your right arm into the block (**25** and **26**);

● Time the movement so that the blocking forearm takes up its final position as the step back comes to a complete stop.

Figures 25 and 26 *The left fist pulls back to the hip while the right forearm continues into the block.*

Rising block uses a rolling action to deflect the opponent's face punch. The blocking forearm travels diagonally upwards across and away from the face, the palm turned to the floor, but as final blocking position is reached the forearm rotates so the little finger side of the fist turns upwards.

The following are common rising block faults to avoid:

- The blocking forearm is too low, so it covers the eyes and deflects the attack into the forehead instead of over the head;

- The blocking forearm travels upwards but not forwards, so there is little safe distance in which to deflect the attack;

- The blocking forearm is to the side of, rather than directly above, the face. This does not sweep the face effectively.

Two additional blocks — this time to the mid-section — are required for the first white belt syllabus. They are performed while advancing or retreating, and the first to be considered is practised as you advance.

Mid-section outer block

- This block is known in Japanese as **chudan soto uke**. Begin by stepping forward from fudodachi. As you do so, begin this sequence: — extend your left fist and raise and bend your right elbow, so the fist comes to lie a fist width from the side of your head (**27**);

- Step directly forward with the right foot. At the same time begin to employ a pulley effect, opening and drawing

Figure 27 *The block begins from a position near the right ear.*

back your left hand while swinging the right forearm forward (**28** and **29**);

- Swing the right forearm across your body as the step comes to a stop and weight settles on the right foot;

- As the blocking fist sweeps across the mid-line of your chest, rotate the forearm so the little finger turns inwards, and link this with a sharp pull-back of the left hip;

Figures 28 and 29 *The blocking forearm swings around in a circular action.*

Figures 30 and 31 *Block so that the deflecting fist is at the height of the shoulder. Note the 90-degree bend in the blocking arm.*

- The blocking fist should now be a fist-width below the chin in terms of height, and there is a 90-degree bend in the elbow (**30** and **31**).

The blocking action is aided by a short muscle spasm which brings into play all the muscles of the body. The legs must not fight against the action of the upper body, so allow the knees to move freely.

The following are the most common mistakes:

- A failure in co-ordination, so the block is made only after forward movement has come to a stop;

- The blocking arm does not move fully across the body, so the opponent's punch can still reach;

36

Figures 32 and 33 *Extend your right arm and fold the left across your chest.*

- The blocking arm moves too far across, so the upper body is turned away;

- The blocking forearm is not sufficiently flexed, so it doesn't sweep a wide area;

- The blocking forearm is over-flexed, so it is too close to the chest;

- The forearm does not rotate in the last

instants, so the block lacks force.

Mid-section inner block

Continue practising until you run out of space, then step back and perform a series of retreating mid-section inner blocks (**chudan uchi uke**). Begin from right forward stance, then follow this sequence:

- Step directly back with the right foot. At the same time extend your right arm

Figures 34 and 35 *As you continue to step forward, withdraw your right arm.*

and open the hand fully, turning it palm-downwards. This is to provide the pulley action. Flex your left elbow and drop the forearm diagonally down and across the lower part of your body, so that the thumb touches the lower right rib cage (**32** and **33**);

- As the step continues, begin to swing the left forearm up and across the body in the manner of a windscreen wiper. Power this action by the pull-back of the right arm (**34** and **35**);

- The step is now virtually complete; the right fist has pulled all the way back to the right hip and the left forearm rotates so the thumb turns outwards;

Figures 36 and 37 *The blocking forearm has described the action of a windscreen wiper.*

The blocking fist is at the same level as the shoulder. There is a 90-degree bend in the elbow, and the outer side of forearm is in line with the side of the body (**36** and **37**).

The block is powered by three actions, only one of which is immediately apparent:

● Shoulder and upper arm muscle action;

● The blocking arm is relaxed throughout and it only tightens as the forearm rotates:

● The whole body spasms as the block makes contact.

The most common mistakes encountered in this technique are:

● A failure in co-ordination, so that the block is made only after forward movement has come to a complete stop;

● The blocking arm does not move fully across the body so the opponent's punch can still reach;

● The blocking arm moves too far across the body;

● The blocking forearm is not sufficiently flexed, so it fails to sweep a wide area;

● The blocking forearm is flexed too much, so there is only a short distance in which to deflect an attacking punch before it strikes;

● The blocking forearm is not rotated at the end of its sweep, so the technique lacks force.

Front kick

Front kick (**maegeri**) employs a snapping action and digs the ball of the foot into the opponent's mid-section. Before you can use this kick, however, you must be able to pull your foot quickly into the correct shape. Practise by standing normally, then raise your heal as high as possible from the floor, so the toes are flexed back and the instep is in line with the shin. Keeping this shape, raise your foot from the floor and point it at the target.

Most novices either fail to pull their toes back, or they flex the ankle joint. The first fault causes toe injuries and the second robs the kick of distance and the ability to resist recoil. It is not necessary or even desirable to keep the kicking foot pulled into shape, since this would slow the kick.

The object is to pull the foot into shape just before impact, but this takes a great deal of practice.

Once you can pull the toes back, practise front kick from a forward stance. Hold both arms well away from your sides and clench the hands into fists. Perform the kick and land forward. When you finally run out of space, perform the final kick and instead of landing forward, withdraw the foot and step back with the kicking leg. You must be able to perform this kick to various heights so we will examine the most difficult of all — front kick to the head (**mae-geri jodan**). Follow this sequence from left forward stance:

● Raise the right foot, bringing the right hip forward. Do not thrust off the ball of the foot, since this produces the wrong foot shape. Lift the foot directly, so that the sole remains parallel to the floor;

● Swing the right knee forward and up, pivoting on the bent supporting leg (**38** and **39**);

● As the knee comes to point at the desired target, straighten the leg and thrust the foot into the target (**40** and **41**);

● Keep control of body weight by slightly leaning back, but not past the point where the back of the head is vertically above the heel of the supporting foot;

● Withdraw your foot promptly after impact is made, otherwise the oppo-

Figures 38 and 39 *Swing the kicking knee forward and up.*

Figures 40 and 41 *Extend the knee and snap the foot out. Lean back slightly to keep control over your centre of gravity.*

nent can seize it and jerk you off balance;

● Set the spent kicking foot down in a forward position so as to set up the next kick.

The effective kick uses one smooth action, rather than a series of separate moves. The novice's front kick suffers from numerous faults, the most common being:

● Opening your groin as you raise the kicking knee. Keep the kicking foot near the side of the supporting leg;

● Failing to raise your kicking knee high enough, so the kick is too low;

● Straightening your supporting leg, so you bob up and down;

● Tensing your shoulders so you hunch up as you kick;

● Waving your arms about as you kick;

● Kicking off-centre;

● Losing control over your centre of gravity so that the kicking foot slams down, not necessarily in the best position.

Sparring

Sparring is introduced early on in the Shotokan syllabus as a way of teaching students how to deal safely with a series of attacks. Both attacker and defender know beforehand what they are going to do and it is just a question of matching size, speed and skill. In the following two forms, we shall look at one prearranged sparring routine dealing with mid-section punches and another which counters punches to the head.

The attacker will perform five successive and identical attacks. The defender withdraws five times and counters each one. This routine is therefore called 'five step sparring', or **gohon kumite** in Japanese. The final counter is followed by a single counter attack. Then attacker and defender change roles and the routine is repeated. Five step sparring is an excellent training aid because it allows both parties to settle into a rhythm before having to break and change roles. However, do realize that this is a very basic form of sparring. It is not meant to simulate an actual free sparring situation.

Five step sparring — mid-section

The first technique uses five mid-section attacks. Let us assume you are taking the role of defender. You will respond to the attacks with the outer block which we practised in the preceding basic technique part of the syllabus. Begin by performing a standing bow (**ritsu rei**) to each other, then step into fudodachi. The attacker draws back his right foot into forward stance and swings his left arm down and across his body in a lower parry. Remain in fudodachi and await his advance (**42**).

The attacker steps forward and performs a lunge punch to your mid-section. Step back with your right leg even as he begins to move forward, and deflect his punch with your left forearm (**43**). There is the briefest of pauses before the attacker steps forward once more. Retreat into right forward stance and block with your right forearm (**44**). Repeat the sequence twice more, then the final attack finds you stepping back with your right leg and blocking with your left forearm (**45**). Pause for an instant, then draw back your left fist to per-

Figure 42 *Remain in fudodachi. Your partner steps back into forward stance.*

Figure 43 *Step back and block your attacker's punch with your left forearm.*

Figure 44 *Take a full step back and block with your right arm.*

Figure 45 *The final step back takes you into left stance.*

Figure 46 *Attack his ribs with a reverse punch.*

Figure 47 *Step back and deflect your attacker's punch with a rising block.*

Figure 48 *Take a full step back and block with your right forearm.*

Figure 49 *The last block finds you in left forward stance and blocking with your left arm.*

form a powerful reverse punch to your opponent's ribs (**46**).

Five step sparring — head

This routine is very similar to the previous one except that all the attacks are made to your face and you respond each time with a rising block. Your attacker steps forward into right forward stance and punches with his right fist. You step back from fudodachi with your right foot and block with your left arm (**47**). Your opponent advances and makes a second punch, which you then block with your right forearm (**48**). Repeat this a further three times so that you block the final punch with your left forearm (**49**).

Pause for an instant, then pull back your left arm and thrust out your right fist in a reverse punch to your opponent's floating ribs (**50**).

This concludes the sparring requirement for 9th kyu.

Kata

You must learn one kata called **Heian shodan** for the 9th kyu grade. Space does not permit a full description of the kata, so all I can do is explain that it takes the basic punches and blocks which you have learned and arranges them into a series of routines. This does three things:

- It improves your skill level by allowing frequent repetitions of basic techiques;

- It teaches you to think in terms of series of movements — not just single techniques;

- When practised with enthusiasm, it increases whole-body endurance and

Figure 50 *Pause for an instant and then deliver a punch to your opponent's floating ribs.*

helps you improve your fitness level.

At first you will be required to perform the kata to a count. This gives you the chance to remember which technique comes next. When you have practised the kata often enough, you will be able to 'forget' the moves themselves and concentrate instead upon the skill of performance.

The grading

After 96 hours or so of training, the average student will be ready to grade. This entails repeating the techniques which you have learned in front of the club coach, or an external grading examiner. You will be called up, perhaps in groups of four or more; some examiners will require you to go right through the syllabus without pause, but more modern coaches are interested in seeing the level of skill reached, not the extent of your physical endurance! They will ask you to perform one section of the syllabus and then give you a rest as another group is called up.

If the examiner is the club coach, he will know your standards and a poor performance on the night may not mean an utter failure. Even when the grading is conducted by an external examiner, the club coach will doubtless be on hand to comment on your usual standard of practice. It is a poor coach indeed who encourages you to take a grading when he believes you do not yet have the required level of skill.

You will be allowed to grade when you have learned all of the techniques. If you are not sure of some, get help well before the date of the examination. Do not try to learn them in the hours before a grading — this time is far better employed composing yourself. Technical ability is one factor in passing a grading; enthusiasm and spirit are others. Most coaches would say 'Better an enthusiastic average karateka than a laid-back elite performer'. Remember this!

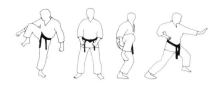

The Second White Belt Syllabus

Introduction

The second white belt syllabus contains only one new basic technique to learn and two new five-step sparring sequences, so by comparison with the requirements for first white belt, 8th kyu is less of a struggle. Having said that, you will be expected to demonstrate a higher level of skill than formerly.

Basic techniques

Begin as for the previous grade with basic punching and reverse punch. If you have forgotten how to do them, now is a good time to refamiliarize yourself. Follow this training with lunge punch, advancing five times then retreating whilst performing rising block. When you have done this, advance and perform mid-section outer block, followed by a retreating mid-section inner block. Practise the advancing front kick, then retreat using knife block from back stance.

Knife block from back stance

Knife block (**shuto-uke** in Japanese) uses the edge of the hand on the little finger side in a wiping action that sweeps the upper chest and face clear. Back stance (**kokutsu dachi**) is particularly suitable for this block because it sets up the shoulders for a powerful action..

Let's begin by looking at the characteristics of this stance:

- Weight is biased towards the rear, and only 30 per cent rests on the front foot. This is achieved by drawing the body back over the rear foot;

- The heels are only an inch or so out of line and the front foot points forward. The rear foot is turned 90 degrees from the front;

- The rear knee is bent more than the front knee yet the body remains perfectly upright. The hips are turned 45 degrees away from forward-facing;

- The front foot, knee and thigh must all be in one straight line.

The following are typical faults:

- Weight bias is incorrect and up to 50 per cent rests on the front foot. Shift the body weight back towards the rear foot;

- The heels are not in the correct line. Check by using a floorboard, taped line, or mirror;

- The hips are not turned correctly, so either the body is square on, or they are turned too far away and the leading knee is pulled inwards.

Set up the stance and feel what it is like to hold the correct position. This will help

Figures 51 and 52 *Weight is biased over the rear foot. The blocking arm inclines forward and the right is turned palm-upwards on the chest.*

you to self-correct as you step from one stance into another. Once you can do this freely, then you are ready to combine it with the blocking action.

Begin from a left back stance with the left foot leading. Bend your left elbow through 90 degrees and bring it inwards slightly, otherwise it will poke out to the side. Turn your left forearm so the palm faces forward, extend your fingers then flex

your thumb across the palm. Bend your right elbow and extend your hand, turning it palm upwards so the fingertips point towards the left elbow (**51** and **52**). Practise taking up back stance with knife block on both left and right sides.

The following are typical faults of knife block:

● The blocking elbow sticks out to the

side. Bring it in line with the side of your chest;

● The right wrist is bent, so the fingers point upwards. Fully extend the wrist joint.

Step forward from a right back stance and as you do:

● Drop your right arm forward, so that the palm faces the floor, and raise your left palm to your right ear (**53** and **54**);

● Slide your front foot to its new position and begin to pull back your right arm,

Figures 53 and 54 *Keep your knees bent to avoid bobbing up and down. Your right arm extends, the left folds over your right shoulder.*

Figures 55 and 56 *Begin to pull back the right arm, using this action to drive the knife block.*

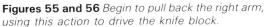

using this action to power the knife block (**55** and **56**);

● Draw your right arm back to your chest whilst cutting outwards and across with the left. Rotate both forearms together, so the left palm turns forward and the right turns upwards (**57** and **58**).

The blocking action is smooth, fast and relaxed. Ensure that it really does sweep across your upper body, otherwise it may allow an attack to pass through. The only

Figures 57 and 58 *Complete the pull back so the right palm turns upwards.*

tension occurs as the forearms rotate and this is followed by immediate relaxation.

When you can perform the block smoothly, practise blocking as you step backwards.

Kumite

The second white belt requires that you perform two additional five-step sparring routines. The first uses a sequence of five attacking punches to mid-section, and the second a sequence to the head. The coach will define the responses made to each. For example, you may be required to demonstrate knife block against a mid-section punch. This requires a little care since forward stance carries the attacker further forward than back stance takes you away, so if you are not careful, he will overstep you at some stage during the routine. This situation is made worse if the attacker is much taller than you.

Figure 59 *Step back and deflect your partner's kick by striking it on the side of the shin. Do not meet the force of the kick full-on with your forearm!*

Figure 60 *Reverse punch even as your partner drops forward — don't wait too long!*

Some schools substitute a front kick attack routine in place of the mid-section punches. If so, you respond with lower parry. You will recall that this is the block you use when stepping into forward stance. Step back as the kick is launched, extending your non-blocking arm to provide the pulley action. Withdraw the non-blocking arm as weight settles and swing your blocking arm down, so it strikes the kick *on the side of the shin* (**59**). It is most important that you do not meet the upswinging shin full-on with your forearm! Repeat the routine five times and conclude with a reverse punch to the attacker's solar plexus (**60**).

Kata

The same kata — **Heian shodan** — is used for 8th kyu as was used for 9th except that this time it is not performed to a count. You are now expected to know the kata, so you should be able to perform it all the way through without hesitation. You begin from fudodachi and, on the command, proceed all the way through — but remain in your last stance and wait to be called back to fudodachi.

Do not make the mistake of thinking that the faster you perform kata, the more marks you will get. Rhythm is more important than sheer speed and the examiner will want to see whether you split the fast from the slow sequences. Do not worry — the coach will show you which is which but, as a rule of thumb, follow blocks with an immediate counter. Then pause and look in the new direction your next advance takes you.

Move at a speed that allows you to show your techniques to advantage. It is better to perform the kata slowly and get it right, than quickly and lose all technique.

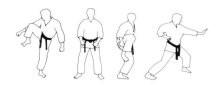

The Yellow Belt Syllabus

Introduction

In addition to the more familiar techniques of the previous two grades, 7th kyu requires two combinations of kick and punch, a high side kick and a new form of pre-arranged sparring. Kata requirement is increased by the introduction of the second basic kata — **Heian nidan**. Both this and **Heian shodan** must be performed for the yellow belt grading.

Basic techniques

The syllabus begins with advancing lunge punch practice. When you run out of space, begin stepping back whilst performing rising block and reverse punch.

Rising block reverse punch

Begin from your last lunge punch stance — in this case right forward stance (**61**) — and follow this sequence:

● Open your right hand but keep the extended arm steady as you take a full

Figure 61 *Begin from right forward stance and extend your right arm.*

53

Figure 62 *Use the pull-back of your right arm to help power a rising block with the left.*

Figure 63 *Then use pull-back of the rising block itself to power the reverse punch.*

step back into left forward stance;

- Use the extended arm to power the pulley action needed to produce a strong block. Draw your right fist back to the hip and perform rising block with your left arm (**62**);

- Use the extended blocking arm in turn to power your reverse punch to mid-section (**63**).

This combination teaches hip action in so far as the rising block is delivered with the punching hip withdrawn (see again **62**). As the punch is made, the hip twists forward and the shoulders follow. Reverse punch does not rely solely upon shoulder action, but also uses the hips to produce power. Note that the position of the feet does not change during the two actions.

Avoid the following mistakes:

- Waving your punching arm about as you step back;

- Failing to open your extended hand before you draw it back. This small detail does give a worthwhile bonus in power when the hand clenches into a fist during the last instants of the blocking action;

- Failing to use your hips correctly, so that the punch is delivered only by pulley and shoulder action;

- Not pausing between the block and the punch, so that one blurs into the other. Pause for an instant between the two.

Mid-section outer block reverse punch

This technique also combines block and reverse punch techniques which we learned in the 9th kyu grade. Begin by revising these two separate techniques and, when you have done so, take up right forward stance and punch with your left arm. Then follow this sequence:

- Advance into left forward stance. As you are doing this, straighten your right arm and extend the fingers, turning the hand palm-downwards. Pull the left fist back to the side of your head;

- Use the extended right arm to power the pulley action that swings your left forearm across your body. In the last instants, the right hand clenches tightly into a fist and the blocking forearm rotates (**64**);

Figure 64 *Block right across your body, twisting your forearm during the last instants.*

- Now use pull-back of the blocking arm and hip action to thrust out a reverse punch (**65**).

Looking at **64** and **65**, you will see the two different hip positions adopted. The block is performed with the right hip pulled well back and the punch is performed with the right hip twisted forward.

Apart from errors in the performance of the block or punch, the only two mistakes to avoid are:

- Failing to use hip action to power the punch;

- Failing to pause for an instant between block and punch.

Mid-section inner block reverse punch

This technique is performed as you step back. Having said that, there is no reason at all why you should not practise it whilst advancing and, for that matter, why you should not practise the previous technique while retreating! However, for the purpose of orderly practice, it is assumed that you have advanced as far as is possible and are in right forward stance, with your left fist extended. Now follow this sequence:

- Step back into left forward stance. As you do so, extend your right arm, opening the hand out and turning the palm downwards. Fold your left arm down across your stomach, so the thumb-side of the fist contacts your right floating ribs;

- Use the extended right arm to power the block, so the left forearm moves up

and across the body in the manner of a windscreen wiper (**66**). Block strongly;

- Pull the blocking arm back to the left hip and drive the right hip forward. Use this combined action to power the reverse punch.

This combination is subject to the same errors as were found in the previous routine.

The syllabus next requires you to practise knife block whilst advancing and retreating. Follow this with front kick practice — also in advancing and retreating modes.

Front kick lunge punch

Revise lunge punch and front kick before beginning practice with this combination. The sequence is performed in the following manner:

- Begin by stepping into left forward stance from fudodachi. Bring your left arm down and across your body in a lower parry (**67**);

- Perform front kick, but keep the punching arm still so that the kick passes to the side of it (**68**);

- Withdraw the kick sharply and set the foot down carefully;

- Pull your left fist back as weight descends on the right heel, using this action to help thrust out a right lunge punch.

Avoid the following mistakes:

- Kicking too low or off-centre;

- Waving the punching arm about dur-

Figure 65 *Use pull-back of the blocking arm to power a reverse punch.*

Figure 66 *Block across your body in the manner of a windscreen wiper.*

ing the kick. The body tends to lean back and this causes the punching arm to rise;

● Hunching up your shoulders as you kick. Keep them relaxed;

● Letting the non-punching arm move away from your side as you kick. Keep it to your side;

● Punching at the wrong time. Perform the punch as weight descends on the front foot. Time it right and you will add your body's momentum to the punch's power. Time it wrongly and you will either throw yourself forward, or you will punch late, robbing it of power.

Figure 67 *Advance into forward stance and perform lower parry.*

Practise this technique in both advancing and retreating modes.

Front kick reverse punch

This is very similar to the preceding technique. Follow this sequence:

● Begin by stepping into left forward stance from fudodachi, then bring your left arm down across your body in a lower parry;

● Perform a reverse punch with your right fist. Notice how this advances the hip and makes the following kick easier (**69**);

Figure 68 *Perform front kick so that the foot passes to the side of the extended arm.*

- Perform front kick with the right leg but keep the punching arm still, so the leg passes to the inside of it (**70**);

- Withdraw the kick and set the foot down carefully, so the hips are 'cocked' ready for the following punch (**71**);

- Pull your right fist back as weight descends on the right heel, using this action to help thrust out a reverse punch (**72**).

Figure 69 *Reverse punch turns the hip forward, making it easier to follow with the kick.*

Figure 70 *The kicking leg extends, passing inside the punching arm.*

Figure 71 *Drop the spent kicking foot so that the hips are 'cocked' ready to deploy the punch.*

Re-read the previous section for common mistakes because they apply here too! In addition, do note that the way you position the spent kicking foot determines the effectiveness of the subsequent reverse punch. Place the foot so that the hips are opened out — this allows the punch to capitalize on both the hip action and the slight forward movement of the body as it settles into forward stance.

Practise this technique also in advancing and retreating modes.

High side snap kick

This interesting kick uses the edge of the foot in a snapping action to your opponent's jaw. Unlike front kick, the ankle is flexed (as when you are standing normally on it). Raise your big toe and turn the others downwards — if you can not manage this at first, then either lift all of your toes, or turn them all downwards. A little practice will soon allow you to form the correct foot position.

High side snapping kick (**keage**) is performed from a straddle stance called **kibadachi**. Practise the stance by stepping to the side from fudodachi, first with the left foot, then with the right. Do not step forward at all — the heels remain in line and the stance is very wide. For obvious reasons some schools call this 'horse-riding stance'. Check off the following points:

● Weight is distributed equally on both feet. The knees are well bent and pushed outwards (**73**);

Figure 72 *Twist the punching hip forward as you perform reverse punch.*

Figure 73 *The stance is wide and the knees are equally bent.*

- The feet are parallel and the back is straight (**74**);
- The fists are clenched and the arms are held away from the body;
- The head is turned in the direction that an advance will be made.

Avoid the following mistakes:

- Allowing the knees to drop inwards;
- Twisting the feet outwards;
- Leaning forwards, or allowing the backside to poke out.

Once you can take up the straddle stance effectively, the next stage is to practise stepping from one stance into another. This action is performed by a sideways movement usually referred to as a 'scissors step'. Take up a straddle stance and turn your head in the direction you wish to advance. Bring the rear foot across the front of the leading, supporting leg, keeping both knees well bent (**75** and **76**) — if you don't, you will appear to bob up and down during the movement. You can also use the scissors action for retreating.

Adjust the length of your step to cover the distance required. With a little practice this movement becomes quite fast and it is possible to use it as an accelerator. The key is always to co-ordinate step and technique, so the latter begins even as the step forward concludes.

Once you can step quickly, take up straddle stance and turn your head to the right. Then follow this sequence:

74

Figure 74 *The back is straight and the backside is not pushed out.*

Figures 75 and 76 *Keep both knees bent as the rear foot scissors steps across the front of the forward leg.*

- Make the scissors step by stepping across the front of your right leg with your left;

- Lift your right foot and form it into the correct shape for the kick (**77** and **78**);

- Lift your right foot in an upswinging arc to strike under the imaginary opponent's chin (**79** and **80**);

Figures 77 and 78 *Raise your kicking knee to the side and form your foot correctly.*

- Withdraw the foot and set it down carefully in a forward straddle position.

Avoid the following mistakes:

- Forming the kicking foot incorrectly, so the flat of the foot swings upwards;

- Allowing the ball of the foot to lead the heel. This usually occurs when the hips

Figures 79 and 80 *Lift your foot in an upswinging arc to your opponent's chin.*

- Losing control over your centre of gravity, so you fall forward after the kick has been delivered.

are not turned fully sideways to the kicking action;

- Not bending the kicking knee, so the action deteriorates into a simple upswing in which the knee plays no part;

- Allowing your arms to wave about. Hold them extended without making the shoulders unnecessarily rigid;

Sparring

For the first time we encounter three step sparring (**sanbon kumite**). This uses three *different* but nevertheless pre-agreed attacks to which the defender responds with three different responses. This system provides a safe introduction to the versatility required in free sparring. The first routine is practised on both left and right sides.

Figure 81 *Take a full step back and deflect your partner's face punch with a rising block.*

Figure 82 *Step back and deflect your opponent's mid-section punch with an inner block.*

Figure 83 *Deflect the front kick by stepping back and performing lower parry.*

Begin from fudodachi. Your partner steps into a left forward stance and brings his left arm down into lower parry position. Then he steps forward and lunge punches to your face. Step back into left forward stance and perform rising block with your left forearm (**81**). After a brief pause, your opponent steps forward and this time uses a lunge punch to mid-section. Step back into right stance and deflect his arm outwards with an inner block (**82**). Your opponent then advances with the final attack and uses a front kick. Step back into left

84

forward stance and deflect his kick with a lower parry (**83**). Finally, perform a reverse punch to your opponent's mid section (**84**).

For this to be effective, the punch must be delivered before your opponent has time to collect his guard. Pause briefly then withdraw a full step from your partner. Pause again, then withdraw into fudodachi.

Kata

The 7th kyu kata is known as **Heian nidan**. This is slightly more advanced than the previous form, but the techniques which it incorporates have now been thoroughly covered and it is only a question of practising them as part of a new routine.

Figure 84 *Perform a reverse punch to your opponent's mid-section.*

The Orange Belt Syllabus

Introduction

The orange belt syllabus introduces two new kicking techniques, some new combinations and the third of the Heian katas.

Basic technique

Three punch sequence

It's all very well having a powerful punch, but what if it misses? Your opponent may be able to block a single punch, but multiple punches place even the best defensive system under considerable pressure, and one slip is all it takes! Furthermore, if each punch is aimed at a different target, life is made even more difficult for the defender. This is the idea behind the 'three punch sequence' (**sanbon zuki**).

Begin from fudodachi and follow this sequence:

- Step into left forward stance and bring your left arm down and across your body in a lower parry (**85**);

- Advance into right forward stance and

Figure 85 *Begin from left lower parry position.*

Figure 86 *Advance into right forward stance and lunge punch to the face.*

Figure 87 *Use the pull-back of the spent fist to power a reverse punch to mid-section.*

lunge punch to the face (**86**);

- Using the pulley principle, draw back the spent lunge punch and use this action to help power a reverse punch to mid-section (**87**);

- Use the spent reverse punch in turn to power a final lunge punch to mid-section (**88**).

Avoid the following mistakes:

- Advancing too slowly into the first punch. Spring forward by thrusting off the rear leg;

- Failing to complete a punch with a focused impact before performing the next punch. There must be the briefest of pauses — but a pause nonetheless — between each of the three punches. It is during this time that the muscles tense up to make the body rigid and the punch powerful;

- Hunching the shoulders as you punch. This is a serious problem which can only be resolved by relaxing the upper body between impacts. If one muscle is fighting against another, then the action will slow and the shoulders will rise.

The key to this routine, which is a feature of all advanced karate technique, is the ability to spasm your muscles on impact and then to immediately and fully relax them.

The basic technique part of the syllabus continues with a return to more familiar routines. Step back from the previous sequence and perform rising block/reverse punch. Advance using outer block/reverse punch and retreat with inner block/reverse punch.

Figure 88 *Then use pull-back of the reverse punch to power a final lunge punch.*

69

Figure 89 *'Spear hand' uses the tips of the fingers in a thrusting action. Use this particular version to attack the opponent's breast bone.*

Figure 90 *Step into left back stance and knife block.*

91

Figure 91 *Slide your left foot to the side; this 'cocks' the hip.*

Knife block, reverse punch, spear hand

This sequence teaches how to move swiftly between stances of a different type. It also introduces a new strike known as 'spear hand' or, in Japanese, **nukite** (**89**). It is delivered by a punching or thrusting action, but the hand extends fully instead of clenching into a fist. The thumb locks across the palm and the fingers stiffen on impact. The index finger is longer than the others, so slightly flex it until the tips of the three longest fingers are in one line.

There is a natural tendency for the fingers to bend on impact, and this can only be prevented through practice against a light and resilient target.

Spear hand can be delivered in two ways. The first is with the thumb upwards (as in **89**), in which case it is typically used to attack the breast bone. The second is delivered from straddle stance with the palm turned downwards, when it is used against the floating ribs or groin.

Begin from fudodachi and follow this sequence:

- Step forward with your left foot and take up back stance. Perform knife block at the same time (**90**);

- Slide your left foot to the side so as to 'cock' the hips ready for the next technique (**91**);

- Perform reverse punch to mid-section (**92**);

- Advance into right forward stance and perform spear hand with your left hand, using the pull-back of your right fist to power it;

- On the next command, rock back on to your rear leg and pull your leading

Figure 92 *Thrust the right hip forward behind the reverse punch.*

Figures 93 and 94 *Practise changing between forward stance and back stance by moving and turning the hips. Allow the leading leg to slide diagonally with each change of stance.*

foot back and inwards. Take up back stance and perform knife block once more.

Practise changing from forward to back stance by drawing the leading foot diagonally back and twisting the hips (**93** and **94**).

Practise the above routine in advancing and retreating mode, then go on to perform

front kick/lunge punch and, afterwards, advancing reverse punch. Withdraw into reverse punch/front kick, then switch to side snapping kick.

Side thrusting kick

This technique uses the same foot position as side snapping kick though it is delivered with a thrusting action. Begin as for snapping kick, by taking up straddle stance (**95**) and stepping across the front of your supporting leg as you advance (**96**). Then follow this sequence:

Figure 95 *Begin from straddle stance and turn your head to look where you are going.*

Figure 96 *Scissors step across the front of your leading leg.*

Figures 97 and 98 *Lift the kicking foot and bring the knee diagonally across the chest.*

Figures 99 and 100 *Thrust your foot out in a straight line. Lean back and look along the full length of your body.*

- Lift your right foot and bring the knee diagonally across your chest (**97** and **98**);

- Thrust your foot out in a straight line to the target and lean back to control your centre of gravity. Allow your supporting foot to rotate up to 180 degrees (**99** and **100**);

- Arch your back and look along the full length of your body and leg. Carry your right arm along the top of the extended leg and flex the left against your chest;

- Withdraw the spent foot, pulling the knee back to your chest. Put the foot down so as to set up an effective stance.

Power for the kicking action comes from the thrusting out of the foot combined with rotation of the hips, and these must flow together without hesitation or jerkiness. For added penetration, drag the supporting foot forward, using momentum generated by the extending leg. This gives a slight bonus in range and soaks up the recoil of impact.

Practise this kick against a heavier punch bag, or against one steadied by a partner. This will show up the effects of recoil and help you to get the correct foot position.

The impact can be made in two ways. The first method (not shown) strikes a jolting blow with the heel. The second extends the foot slightly to produce a slicing action using the little toe edge of the foot (see again **100**).

The following are common faults:

- Hesitating between bringing up the knee and thrusting out the kick;

75

Figures 101 and 102 *Lift your kicking leg to the side of your body. This movement requires good hip flexibility.*

- Not twisting sufficiently on the supporting foot, so range and penetration are lost. Maximum thrust is developed when the hips are turned fully sideways to the opponent;

- Not arching the back correctly, so penetration is lost;

- Not raising the kicking knee high enough, so the foot swings upwards in the manner of a side snapping kick, instead of thrusting out horizontally;

- Failing to lean back, so the used kick thumps down willy-nilly;

- Not forming the kicking foot correctly,

so the sole of the foot strikes the target. Lead with the edge of the foot or heel.

Learn how to perform side thrusting kick whilst advancing and retreating.

Roundhouse kick

This is a very common kick which can be delivered either with the ball of the foot or with the toes pointing — traditionally the

Figures 103 and 104 *Swivel on your supporting foot and drive the ball of your foot into the target.*

former version is learned first. As its name implies, roundhouse kick travels along a horizontal and circular path, striking the target from the side. Do not use this kick to attack facing targets; attack the ribs, or the side of the jaw instead. The Japanese name for this techique is **mawashigeri**.

Begin from left forward stance, then follow this sequence:

● Lift your right foot, pull back your toes, and pivot outwards on the supporting foot;

● Lift your right knee upwards, forward *and outwards* in one fluid movement (**101** and **102**);

● Continue to turn so that your right side faces your opponent. This helps to draw the kicking hip around, so the right knee is brought across the front of the body. The supporting leg has pivoted by at least 90 degrees at this stage;

● Thrust the right foot out horizontally as the knee is about to reach maximum height (**103** and **104**);

Figure 105 *Step back and deflect your partner's punch with a rising block.*

Figure 106 *Step back a second time and perform inner block.*

Figures 107 and 108 *Slide your foot back as you see the kick developing and use your right arm in a reverse lower parry.*

- Tighten the lower leg muscles as the foot is about to make contact, then pull it back before your opponent can seize hold of it;

- Put the foot down in such a way as to set up an effective forward stance.

The following are common faults of round-house kick:

- The supporting leg does not rotate. This prevents the hips from acting properly;

- The kicking knee does not lift high enough, so the kick is too low. Sometimes the student tries to compensate for this by over-rotating the hips, which causes the kicking knee to face down to the floor and makes matters worse!

- The kicking foot does not tense on impact. Pull the toes back to reduce the risk of ankle injury;

- Control over the centre of gravity is lost and the kicking foot virtually falls to the floor.

Perform this technique in advancing and retreating modes.

Sparring

A new three step sparring routine is practised for this grade. It begins from fudo-dachi with your opponent stepping forward and attacking with a punch to the face. Step back and deflect the attack with rising block (**105**). After the briefest of pauses, the opponent advances again but this time performs a lunge punch to mid-section. Step back again and perform inner block (**106**). The opponent then uses front kick which you deflect by stepping back and blocking with the same arm which you used for the previous inner block. This technique is sometimes called 'reverse lower parry' because it is delivered with the opposite arm and leading leg (**107** and **108**).

Draw back your blocking arm and use this action to thrust out a punch to the opponent's face (**109**). This action also

Figure 109 *Draw back the blocking arm, using this action to power a punch to the face.*

benefits by the action of the hips as they twist back from the blocking position to forward stance. Complete the sequence with a reverse punch to the opponent's mid-section (**110**). This is powered in part by the pull-back of the left fist.

Kata

Kata requirement for 6th kyu is **Heian san-dan**, plus one of the previous two.

Figure 110 *Pull back the spent punch and use this action to power a final reverse punch to mid-section.*

The Green Belt Syllabus

Introduction

There are no new techniques to learn in the green belt syllabus (5th kyu) though in some cases previously learned techniques will be put together in new ways. The format of sparring changes to one step routines, and more will be said of this in the relevant section. Kata requirement is the fourth basic kata (**Heian yondan**), plus one other.

Basic techniques

Begin with the three punch sequence in advance and retreating modes, then practise an advancing rising block/reverse punch routine. Step back and perform outer block, elbow strike and back fist.

Outer block, elbow strike and back fist

The Japanese name for this technique is **soto uke/empi/uraken**. Begin from right forward stance with the left fist fully extended. Then follow this sequence:

Figure 111 *Bring your left forearm across your body in an outer block.*

- Step back with your right leg, into forward stance;

- As you step, extend your right arm and open your hand, turning it palm-downwards. Bring your left fist close to the side of your head;

- Co-ordinate the step back so that even as it comes to a stop, the right arm is drawn strongly back and the left swings across the body in an outer block (**111**);

- Rock back on to your right foot and draw the left back and inwards. Open your blocking hand and fold the arm back and across the front of your chest (**112**);

- Thrust forward with your right foot and drive the point of your left elbow into your opponent's mid-section. Turn your hips sideways on as you do this and take up straddle stance (**113**);

- Bring your left forearm up and over in a circular motion that snaps the back of the fist into the bridge of the opponent's nose (**114**). This technique is called 'back fist' because it uses the back of the knuckles in a swinging strike. The wrist remains relaxed throughout and impact is made with a snapping action of the forearm that tilts the knuckles into the face.

This is a sophisticated routine, requiring the ability to change fluidly between stances. Avoid the following errors:

- Failing to change stance between the block and elbow strike, so the straddle stance has a side step. You must turn your hips fully, otherwise the strike will be weak. Allow the leading foot to slide into a correct position;

- Failing to open out then clench tightly the arm delivering the elbow strike. This spasm action is essential, otherwise the elbow strike will lack power;

- Keeping the elbow joint and wrist stiff, which shows the back fist.

Knife block, spear hand

The Japanese name for this routine is **shuto uke nukite**, and it follows on immediately from the previous sequence. Take up back stance and advance into a knife block (**115**). Slide your leading foot to the side and pull back your left arm. Use this action to help thrust out spear hand to your opponent's mid-section (**116**).

Figure 112 *Open your left hand and fold it across your chest.*

Figure 113 *Turn your hips sideways on and take up straddle stance. Thrust your left elbow into your opponent's ribs.*

Figure 114 *Snap the back of your left knuckles into the bridge of your opponent's nose.*

Figure 115 *Advance into knife block from back stance.*

Figure 116 *Step to the side and thrust out a spear hand to your opponent's breast bone.*

Inner block, snap punch, reverse punch

This routine is performed in retreating mode. Its Japanese name is **uchi uke kizame zuki gyaku zuki**. Begin from left forward stance with right spear hand extended, then follow this sequence:

- Take a full step back into right forward stance. Extend your left arm and open the hand, turning it palm-downwards. At the same time, drop your right arm across your stomach, so the thumb-side contacts your left floating ribs;

- Strongly pull back your left arm and use this to power an inner block with the right;

- Pause briefly, then thrust down with your left leg so that your body weight is projected forward. Extend your right fist at the same time and deliver a snapping punch to your opponent's face (**117**);

- Develop a pulley action by withdrawing the snap punch quickly and twisting forward with the left hip. Use this to power a reverse punch (**118**).

Follow this routine with reverse punch performed in advancing mode. Retreat with reverse punch/front kick, then practise front kick and lunge punch in both advancing and retreating modes. Go on to perform roundhouse kick and follow this with roundhouse kick, reverse punch.

Roundhouse kick, reverse punch

The Japanese name for this routine is **mawashigeri gyaku zuki**. Begin from right

Figure 117 *Thrust hard with your left leg and perform a snap punch to your opponent's face.*

84

Figure 118 *Pull your right arm back strongly and perform a reverse punch to mid-section.*

Figure 119 *Perform a roundhouse kick to mid-section.*

forward stance and follow this sequence:

- Swivel on your supporting leg and perform a roundhouse kick to mid-section (**119**);

- Withdraw the kick by flexing the knee;

- Set the foot down so the hips are 'cocked' (**120** and **121**);

- Perform a reverse punch to mid-section.

This sequence works properly when the spent kick is set down correctly. The punching hip must be drawn back, otherwise it cannot be projected into the punch and power is lost.

This routine is followed by a side snapping kick and side thrusting kick.

Combination kicks

Combination kicks are known as **rengeri**, and they increase versatility in selecting and using series of kicks. The first example is a two-stage routine combining front kick

Figures 120 and 121 *Set the spent kicking foot down in such a way as to 'cock' the hips prior to the following punch.*

and side thrusting kick (**maegeri kekomi**). Begin from left forward stance and follow this sequence:

- Perform front kick (**122**);

- Withdraw the spent kick and set it down in a forward position;

- Twist on the supporting leg and perform side thrusting kick, so the foot slices across the opponent's front (**123**);

- Set the foot down carefully and take up a new forward stance.

Figure 122 *Perform front kick, then set the spent foot down in a forward position.*

Combinations of kicks often cause the arms to wave about, so hold them relaxed yet firm throughout. There is also a tendency for the supporting legs to straighten so that the sequence takes on a bobbing action. Each kick must be performed properly and completely before the next begins.

Sparring

The green belt syllabus introduces basic sparring routines which use a single attack, and they are known in Japanese as **kihon kumite**. These attacks take the form of either punches to the mid-section and head, or kicks; each person knows the attack to be made because it is specified beforehand. Basic sparring is performed in left and right postures and a different response must be made from each.

There are many possibilities and the following are just some examples:

- Your opponent advances into left forward stance. Remain in fudodachi until he steps forward to attack;

- The opponent steps forward and performs lunge punch. Step into back stance and block his arm with a thrusting knife block. Bring your right hand to the side of your head, as though saluting (**124**);

- Use your right hand to perform knife hand strike to the opponent's collar bone (**125**).

The second sequence is rather more elaborate. Begin as before, and as your

Figure 123 *Pivot on your supporting foot and perform a side thrust kick.*

Figure 124 *Deflect your opponent's punch with a thrusting knife hand, and draw your right hand back to the side of your head.*

Figure 125 *Transfer body weight forward and strike to your opponent's neck with knife hand.*

Figure 126 *Step back and deflect your opponent's face punch with a double rising block (sometimes called an 'x-block').*

Figure 127 *Take your opponent's arm to the right and withdraw your left fist to the hip.*

Figure 128 *Set up your range and then perform a roundhouse kick to mid-section.*

Figure 129 *Withdraw the spent kick and set it down so your back is turned to your opponent.*

opponent punches, follow this sequence:

- Step back into left forward stance and deflect his punch upwards using a double rising block (often called an 'x-block') performed with hands open (**126**);

- Take his arm to your right and withdraw your left fist to the hip (**127**);

- Pivot on your supporting leg and perform roundhouse kick with your right foot to his mid-section, keeping hold of his forearm (**128**);

- Withdraw the spent kick and set it down so your hips are turned and your back is towards your opponent (**129**);

- Release your opponent's forearm and cross your arms in front of your chest (**130**). The purpose of this is to provide a pulley action to help power the following elbow strike;

Figure 130 *Cross your forearms to set up the pulley action needed to power the final technique of this routine.*

Figure 131 *Draw back your right arm and perform a backwards-travelling elbow strike with your left.*

Now follow this sequence:

- Step back into right forward stance and perform an x-block with your closed fists (**132**). It is essential that you allow your forearms to slide easily over each other because this allows the force of impact to be safely absorbed. It is also essential that you close your fists tightly;

- The block drops the opponent's foot to the floor. Withdraw your blocking arms and rotate them so the palms turn upwards. Extend your fingers (**133**);

- Straighten your elbows and thrust both forearms in a double knife strike to your opponent's neck (**134**). The hand edges make a slicing impact. It is essential that you control this technique carefully to avoid causing serious injury to your partner.

All double blocks suffer from the obvious

Figure 132 *Block your opponent's front kick with an x-block, allowing your forearms to slide so that the impact energy is soaked up gradually.*

- Turn your hips and pull your right fist back to the hip. Drive your left elbow back into the opponent's ribs (**131**).

Perhaps the most difficult part of this routine is ranging the roundhouse kick. This you do by positioning your left leg first, but be prepared to withdraw it slightly from your opponent otherwise you may find that you are too close to him.

The final two examples show how to adapt this method of sparring to kicking attacks. In the first routine, the opponent performs a front kick with his right foot.

Figure 133 *Pull both arms back and cross them in front of your chest, opening out the fingers.*

Figure 134 *Straighten your elbows and thrust both hands into a double strike at your opponent's neck.*

Figure 135 *Step diagonally and deflect your opponent's side thrust kick with a reverse lower parry.*

disadvantage of using both arms to do one job. There is also a risk that the opponent will capitalize on his fall forward and thrust out a strong snap punch into your face!

The final example shows a defence against side thrust kick. The attacker has kicked with his right leg. Now follow this sequence:

- Step diagonally forward with the left leg and deflect the kick with a reverse lower parry (**135**).

- Draw up your right foot and raise the knee. Perform a side thrust kick to the back of your opponent's neck (**136**);

- Use the weight of the falling leg to power an elbow strike to your opponent's back (**137**). The hips are already turned sideways on, so the logical stance to take up is a straddle.

Kata

The Kata requirement for 5th kyu is **Heian yondan** plus one of those already learned.

Figure 136 *Draw up your left leg and perform a side thrust kick to the back of your opponent's head.*

Figure 137 *Use the weight of the descending leg to help power an elbow strike to your opponent's back.*

The Purple Belt Syllabus

Introduction

The purple belt syllabus introduces no new basic techniques though it does broaden your knowledge of basic sparring by introducing a greater variety of responses to attack. **Heian godan** is the last of the basic katas.

Basic technique

Begin by advancing into three punch sequence. Withdraw whilst performing three punch sequence/front kick.

Rising block, reverse punch, lower parry

The Japanese name for this routine is **age uke gyaku zuki gedan barai**. Perform it in advancing and retreating modes. Begin from right forward stance, extending the left arm down in a lower parry. Then follow this sequence:

- Advance into left forward stance and perform a rising block (**138**);

Figure 138 *Advance into forward stance and perform rising block.*

Figure 139 *Draw back your left forearm and perform reverse punch to mid-section.*

Figure 140 *Rest the little finger side of your left fist on top of your right shoulder.*

- Use the pull-back of the rising block together with hip action to produce a powerful reverse punch (**139**);

- Fold your left arm so the little finger side of the fist rests on top of your right shoulder (**140**);

- Pull your right fist back to the hip and use this action to help power a lower parry with your left arm (**141**).

Follow this routine with an outer block, elbow, back fist sequence. Then perform inner block, snap punch and reverse punch.

Knife block, front leg front kick, spear hand

The Japanese name for this technique is **shuto uke kizame geri nukite**. Take up

Figure 141 *Pull back your right arm and perform a lower parry with your left.*

Figure 142 *Lift your front foot and snap kick to your opponent's mid-section. Maintain your knife block as you do so.*

knife block from left back stance, then follow this sequence:

- Rock back on your right foot so that the weight comes off your front leg;

- Lift your leading foot and snap kick to your opponent's mid-section (**142**). Maintain your knife hand block;

- Set your left foot down in a forward position and thrust out right spear hand. On the next command, step forward (or back) into the next knife block position.

Advance with reverse punch, then step back whilst performing reverse punch/front kick. Step forward to practise roundhouse kick, then step back and perform round-

95

house kick/reverse punch. Follow this with side snap kick and side thrust kicks, both performed in advancing and retreating modes.

Sparring

Basic sparring requires new responses to head and mid-section punches, to front kick and to side thrusting kick. It also requires two responses to roundhouse kick. The following is one such response:

- Your opponent attacks with roundhouse kick. Step back into left forward stance and deflect the kick with left inner block (**143**);

- Use the pull-back of the block to power a reverse punch, which must land even as the opponent sets his foot down

Figure 143 *Step back and block the roundhouse kick with left inner block.*

Figure 145 *If necessary, draw back your left foot to set the range, then front kick to the opponent's mid-section.*

Figure 144 *Use reverse punch before the opponent has a chance to recover from the failed kick.*

(**144**). If you find that you are too close, use vertical punch (**tate zuki**). This shares the same hip action with reverse punch but the distance travelled is shorter and the fist does not rotate palm-down;

● Complete the technique by drawing back your leading foot to set the range accurately, then front kick to your opponent's mid-section (**145**).

Kata

Kata requirement for 4th kyu is the last of the Heians — **Heian godan**. This, plus any of the previous ones, must be performed.

The First Brown Belt Syllabus

Introduction

The 3rd kyu syllabus is the first of the brown belt grades, and is often distinguished by a wavy white line running through the centre of the belt. Virtually all the basic techniques have now been learned, though one new kick is introduced. The principles of combining techniques into a routine are well established by now, so there is little point in spending a lot of time on the new routines.

From this point onwards, techniques are practised in a more practical format. Sparring continues to increase in degrees of freedom, culminating in unprogrammed free practice. Kata requirement changes as students move away from the basic Heians and into the more advanced katas.

Basic techniques

Begin by advancing into the three punch sequence. Withdraw and perform three punch sequence/front kick. Begin from right forward stance, stepping back to perform three fast punches. The last punch leaves you in left forward stance with the

Figure 146 *Keep your punching fist extended as you kick.*

left fist extended. Keep this punch extended and front kick with the rear leg (**146**).

99

Figure 147 *Shift your weight back over your rear foot and perform roundhouse kick with your front leg. Maintain your guard.*

Figure 148 *Set the spent foot down and thrust out a right spear hand.*

Return the kicking foot to its rearward position once more and make ready to step back again.

Perform rising block, back fist and reverse punch in both advancing and retreating mode. Then practise outer block, elbow, backfist and reverse punch. Inner block, snap punch and reverse punch is performed in both directions, as is knife block, front foot snap kick and spear hand.

Knife block, front foot roundhouse kick, spear hand

The Japanese name for this routine is **shuto uke kizame mawashigeri nukite**. Take up knife block from left back stance, then follow this sequence:

● Rock back on your right foot, so the weight comes off your front leg;

● Lift your leading, left foot and perform roundhouse kick to your opponent's mid-section, maintaining your knife hand block (**147**);

Figures 149 and 150 *Twist your hips so that the front foot draws diagonally back. Turn your back to your opponent but keep your eyes on him.*

- Set your left foot down in a forward position and thrust out a right spear hand (**148**).

Practise reverse punch, front kick and three punch sequence in advance and retreating mode. Then do the same for reverse punch, roundhouse kick and three punch sequence. Follow this with side snap kick and side thrust kicks, both performed in advancing and retreating modes. Combine front kick and roundhouse kick into an advancing routine. Then step back into a front kick/side thrust kick combination.

Back kick to mid-section

Begin from left forward stance and follow this sequence:

- Twist your hips so you turn your back fully on your opponent, but keep your eyes on him at all times. Note how your front foot slides diagonally inwards (**149** and **150**);

Figures 151 and 152 *Lift your kicking foot.*

Figures 153 and 154 *Thrust the foot directly backwards with the heel leading.*

- Lift your right foot (**151** and **152**) and thrust it directly backwards, with the heel leading (**153** and **154**);

- Lean forward but keep your head raised and your arms under control;

- Withdraw the spent kick (**155**) and put your right foot down so as to set up an effective fighting stance.

The following are general faults:

- Not turning your hips enough, so the kick is off-centre;

- Turning your hips too far, so the kick is once again off-centre;

Figure 155 *Withdraw the spent kick and set it down carefully.*

- Letting your arms flap about;
- Failing to lean forward, so the kick is too low;
- Not keeping your eyes on your opponent;
- Not setting your foot down correctly afterwards, so the final stance is badly set up;
- Failing to perform the turn-kick-turn as a smooth sequence.

Sparring

Traditionally in western schools, this is the point at which free sparring (**jiu kumite**) is introduced. However, skill varies according to the individual and, in my opinion, free sparring should not be practised until you have developed control and can form your techniques properly. Most karate injuries occur during free sparring and it is therefore ludicrous to attempt it until you have sufficient skill.

The following rules for free sparring are offered for your consideration:

- The best benefits accrue when both partners are not collapsing from fatigue. Tiredness increases the chances of misjudgement and leads to poor techniques;
- Sparring should not go on and on. Two minutes of actual sparring is optimum. Use a stopwatch to measure elapsed time;
- Do not spar on concrete or tiled surfaces because falling on these can cause serious injury;
- Do not wear spectacles and be extra

careful if you use contact lenses. These are prone to pop out in the hurly-burly;

- Remove earrings, necklaces and sharp-edged rings because these can cause injury both to the wearer and to the partner. Tie long hair back with an elastic band — not with a metal clasp! — and make sure finger and toe nails are both clean and short;

- Men should wear an approved design of groin protector and women should use a breast shield. Fist mitts must be worn. Shin/instep protectors save bruises and give confidence;

- Spar at half speed but do not abuse this and seize hold of your partner's slowed-down kick. Try to touch the opponent lightly on target areas and avoid kicks to his groin, knees and insteps;

- Do not make open-hand attacks to the face or strike at the throat;

- Disengage momentarily when your opponent scores on you, recognize his effort with a nod and then resume sparring. By this means, sparring does not turn into a mêlée of blows and kicks.

- Pull back if things get out of hand and bow to your opponent. Then withdraw from the fighting area.

Prearranged sparring sequences continue alongside free sparring and the required routines will be demonstrated by the coach.

Kata

Kata requirement for 3rd kyu is the curious **Tekki shodan**. This is the first of two related katas characterized by peculiar crab-like sideways movements. Various explanations have been offered to account for this. Generally it is claimed that the two katas represent a method of fighting to be used when there is no possibility of stepping forward or back, but I find this unconvincing.

It seems more likely that they have simply been taken from an earlier kata that has since been lost. They do use complex concurrent arm actions which are characteristic of Southern Shaolin kung fu, but whether this is a case of parallel development or derivation I couldn't say!

The Second and First Brown Belt Syllabus

Introduction

The 2nd and 1st kyu are the final two gradings before black belt. There is generally a six month gap between each, during which time you are expected to improve any slightly deficient techniques. Emphasis has now shifted away from the mechanical performance of basic technique towards the demonstration of skill. Both 2nd kyu and 1st kyu gradings require the kata **Bassai dai**, together with another kata of the examiner's choice.

Second kyu introduces the **jiu ippon** prearranged sparring routines. These are similar to the **ippon kumite** which we have already studied except that they begin from a free fighting posture.

Free fighting posture is known by its Japanese name of **jiu dachi**. It is a non-polarized stance, which means that there is no weight bias over either leg. This allows fast movements in a variety of directions.

Begin from fudodachi by stepping a pace forward with your left foot. Settle your weight evenly between your feet and raise your left hand. Carry it well forward into the projected centre-line of your body, where it can stop an attack close to source. The right fist is carried across the front of the stomach, where it provides a second line of defence and from which position a reverse punch can be quickly deployed. The feet are parallel and both knees are bent (**156**).

Figure 156 *The free fighting stance is unpolarized so it can be used for a variety of purposes.*

When set up correctly, free fighting posture presents the smallest target to the opponent commensurate with your having the maximum possibilities for launching an attack.

Competition

Karate competition is an important if over-stressed part of karate practice. A great many poor coaches have contributed to the widely held misconception that competition is somehow a measure of your ability to practise karate. It is not. It is merely a measure of your ability to practise competition karate. Other aspects of practice are at least as important.

Nevertheless, karate competition cannot be ignored and the following synopsis from the rules may serve as a basic introduction:

- Karate competition can involve both sparring and kata performance;

- There are both individual and team events;

- Team sparring is single sex and uses five men and two reserves, or three women and one reserve. Team kata is also single sex and fields three men or three women;

- Individual sparring bouts last for two minutes of actual fighting time, though senior male bouts may be extended to three minutes;

- A bell or buzzer warns the competitors when there are 30 seconds left and when time has expired;

- The object is to land a controlled and technically good technique on the opponent's body or head. Excellent techniques receive one point score and those which are slightly imperfect merit a half point;

- The bout is won when either contestant scores points and/or half points which total three points. If neither competitor scores the full three points, then the bout will be given to the one with the higher points score. If this is equal, then a decision may be made on the relative fighting abilities. Team matches are decided by the team that has won the most bouts. If this is equal, then the points of each bout are added up. If the tie persists, then a deciding bout is fought;

- Draws are permitted in team matches but individual bouts must produce a winner. A tie-breaking extension bout is fought and the first to score in it wins the match;

- Scores are awarded by a referee and he is assisted by a judge. Both are free to move within the competition area;

- The referee can issue warnings, impose penalties and disqualify those competitors who break the rules. Penalties take the form of half or full points added to the opponent's score. Most common rule infringements are:

1 failing to control the force of a technique, so that the opponent is injured, and
2 stepping outside the match area;

- Kata matches are held over three rounds. The first round selects the 16 best performers, the second round selects 8 and the final round produces the winner;

- Scores are awarded for kata performance by four judges and a chief judge. The highest and lowest scores are deleted and the others are added together. In the event of a tie, the lowest scores are added back in. If the tie persists, then the highest scores are added in. If it still continues, then the two competitors must perform a tie-breaker kata;

- Each competitor selects a kata from an official list of 16 which may be performed. A different kata from the list may be performed in the second round. The third round allows a completely free choice of kata.

Glossary

(Words are arranged in the approximate order of their appearance in training)

Rei Bow

Seiza Kneel

Sensei ni rei Bow to the teacher

Kiritsu Stand up

Nori Stand with heels together, hand flat on thighs

Yoi (fudodachi) Stand with feet apart and hands closed into fists

Kihon Basic punches and strikes

Kara zuki Basic punch

Zenkutsu dachi Forward stance

Oi zuki Lunge punch

Jodan Upper chest, face and head

Chudan Chest and stomach

Gedan Lower stomach and groin

Mawatte Turn

Age uke Rising block

Kiai Shout

Gyaku zuki Reverse punch

Gedan barai Lower parry

Yamei Draw back to fudodachi

Keri (Geri) Kicks

Maegeri Front kick

Surikomi maegeri One step front kick

Keage High snapping side kick

Kekomi Side thrusting kick

Mawashigeri Roundhouse kick

Rengeri Combining kicks together into a routine

Uke Blocks

Chudan soto uke Midsection outer block

Chudan uchi uke Midsection inner block

Shuto uke Knife block

Gohon kumite Five step prearranged sparring

Sanbon zuki Three punch sequence

Sanbon kumite Three step prearranged sparring

Ippon kumite One step prearranged sparring

Empi Elbow

Tate zuki Vertical punch

Uraken Back fist

Heian A series of elementary karate kata

Kata A series of combination techniques and individual basic techniques performed in series to a pre-set order

Nukite Spear hand

Surikomi mawashigeri One step roundhouse kick

Kizame zuki Snap punch

Kizame geri Front kick delivered by leading leg

Ushirogeri Back thrust kick

Jiu kumite Free sparring

Mawashigeri jodan Roundhouse kick to head

Kihon kumite Basic sparring